BE INVIGORATED

THIS IS A NONFICTION BOOK BASED ON STUDIES GATHERED FROM OTHER BOOKS/VIDEOS ON INDO-PAKISTANI WAR OF 1971, FIRST FIELD MARSHAL SAM MANEKSHAW, APJ ABDUL KALAM, AND VEER MARATHA CHHATRAPATI SHIVAJI.

PARMESH K. BATULKAR

I dedicate this book to all Indians.

Contents

Preface

The following Book is based on studies gathered from other books/videos. This Book is made solely for educational purposes.

And if you like, you can give back by doing what you love, living your dreams, and giving your gifts to the world knowing that it will come back to you in incredible ways.

CHAPTER ONE

Partition

When India and Pakistan got partitioned in 1947 at that time, Pakistan had two parts West Pakistan and East Pakistan.

What you are seeing today Bangladesh was not Bangladesh earlier but it was East Pakistan at that time.

Conflicts of East and West Pakistan

The people of East Pakistan spoke Bengali language. The people of Pakistan used to talk about these people in a very joking way, you guys are donkeys, don't know anything, are worth nothing, and are worthless, you guys are small meaning on the contrary, it's a straight joke.

People of West Pakistan did not like East Pakistanis. Tit for tat happened in 1970. In 1970, Sheikh Mujibur Rahman of East Pakistan won the election and he won the election for the post of Prime Minister.

Now what did the army of West Pakistan do, they were not getting him to undertake the pledge. That's why after winning the 1970 election Sheikh Mujibur Rahman sees that it is like this. So he gave his speech on 7th March 1971 and said that now we will make East Pakistan a separate country which will be named Bangladesh.

Due to this speech, the Pakistan Army arrested Sheikh Mujibur Rahman and tied up in West Pakistan on March 25, 1971 and started committing atrocities in East Pakistan.

In protest against the arrest of Sheikh Mujibur Rahman, a rebel group named Mukti Bahini was formed. But the people of West Pakistan committed such terrible atrocities on East Pakistan that in East Pakistan the people of West Pakistan cut three million people. Four lakh women had been raped. Four lakh women of their own country were raped that scene is so outlandish. Can you imagine their cruelty? They committed so much cruelty in their own country with these people after the arrest of Sheikh Mujibur Rahman.

The result of the oppression was that till April 1971, people fled from here in India. Here 10 lakh people came to India to take shelter. So former Prime Minister, Indira Gandhi knew that these people could not go back until there was peace in East Pakistan. And the only way of peace was to support East Pakistan so that the people of West Pakistan can improve.

Helping Hand from Bharat/India

So Prime Minister Indira Gandhi talked to General Field Marshal Manekshaw on this. She told Army Chief Manekshaw that you fight now, we order you to fight now in East Pakistan. We will not leave our neighbors to die like this.

General Field Marshal Manekshaw said that we will not attack because you are not looking at the month it is the month of April, the meaning of the month of April is a rainy day and what is the condition of the east during the rainy season, suddenly the external flood comes. West Pakistan will remain dry and China's area will remain dry, they will attack. We will have to fight from all three sides.

General Field Marshal Manekshaw explained to Indira Gandhi; she understood and asked for how long we will not fight, Manekshaw said till November. But in the middle of April to November, we can train our soldiers to fight in East Pakistan and we can train Mukti Bahini. Andin 1971 our agreement between India and Russia was signed.

Now we had made Pakistan sit on a pile of gunpowder. It was only a matter of waiting that there was a spark in that gunpowder and then Pakistan would have been destroyed. See the coincidence, Pakistan itself lit the spark on the pile of gunpowder.

Our main motive was not war with Pakistan; our main motive was to protect our own Bangladeshi brothers who were being oppressed, whose sisters were being raped. The Pakistanis did so terrible that they raped the daughter in front of the father and later beat the father and said that you also do. All humanity had been destroyed over there.

So India said that we will be less aggressive with West Pakistan. Pakistan got the news that India is weak here. Look, we were waiting for the winter at that time Pakistan made a mistake. He made a surprise attack on 3 December 1971, attacking Srinagar, Pathankot, Chandigarh, and Agra Airport.

Pakistan did such a terrible attack by the Air Force on India that India kept viewing. Pakistan's Air Force ships entered India. Such was the attack, so much that not a single soldier of India was killed.

Do you understand how much external attack happened? Brother, if you enter here, what will happen in our country? India was waiting for this. Brother, we were only planning to attack that you should attack us first. Now even the pressure of the world will not come on us. Brother you have initiated, now we will end. We had made a firm decision. Meanwhile, Pakistan got dangerous news, what was the news brother? Pakistan got the news that most of India's army is more deployed towards East Pakistan. And here is a place in Jaisalmer district of Rajasthan, Longewala. There are only 120 soldiers in that

Longewala. And Pakistan thought that if we kill 120 soldiers overnight, then the Air Force could not fight in the night.

That's why they did the entry in Longewala; they carried a whole terrible tank, took the army, took the infantry and entered Longewala. And India had only 120 soldiers in Longewala. Only 120 and above there were thousands in numbers. But one should not panic because the number of ants cannot drag the sugarcane. Kuldip Singh Chandpuri covered the duty that was in Longewala, Kuldip Singh Chandpuri is Sardar, and now Kuldip Singh is Punjabi Sikh. Now these people do not think anything below 1.25 lakh.

"चड़ियेंसेमैंबाजलडाऊं, गीदडोंकोमैंशेरबनाऊं।"

"सवा लाख से एक लडाऊं तभी गोबिंद सिंह नाम कहाउ!!"

News spread that Brigadier Tariq Mir is coming to fight with you from Pakistan. He has tanks, 2800 army and is coming very fast. You have only 120 soldiers, Kuldip Singh you back off. You are brave, no doubt in this but how do you fight with such a terrible army. He said we are Khalsa Sikh, we cannot move back. We'll show that 120 soldiers will overpower them. They didn't have any resources to blow up the tank. There was a small stall on a jeep to kill the tank and they had only three mines. Then they thought to put three original mines in an empty desert and the food that is eaten in tiffin was laid overnight by these people in lines.

When the tank of Pakistan came, in the beginning it was the original mines, the tank of Pakistan was blown away. One tank of Pakistan blew up, and then another, then the third too was blown. Now Pakistanis are all scared, Brigadier Tariq Mir said brother; these people have kept mines here, call the engineer and take out the whole mines.

It was our Major Kuldip Singh who knew that if we stop Pakistan overnight, our Air Force will come in the morning. That's why they had spread the whole tiffin. These Pakistanis took six hours to get them out. The engineers removed the tiffin out of fear. Actually, our soldiers had filled the tiffin with brick and stones. Their engineers said run away, run away mines are there. These people spent the whole night removing it, taking it out. It was three o'clock in the morning and they saw complete silence. At three o'clock brother, this is tiffin, and we have tiffin in the desert, now they ordered an attack. So Kuldip Singh had made a sandpit in the middle of the desert and had spread his soldiers in an area of 2 km. One from there, one from here, there was firing from all around. Pakistanis thought that we have got wrong information, 120 soldiers will not kill such because bullets were being fired from all sides, bomb blasts all going on, so terrible somewhere 120 men will do like this. No brother, who is killing from where in such a terrible deserted area, completely ruined.

Pakistan is a spoiled child, beaten with love. Dashed Pakistan's tank, then Indian soldiers were standing and taking pictures. There was no selfie at that time, to take a photo from the front, photos that will inspire generations to come.

Tell me Pakistani came with such a beautiful tank, Pakistan brought to kill us; the poor are killed. Major Sir, you also, it's a child, beat the baby with ease.

See it's a bit spoiled child, oof oh shouldn't have beat like that. But what will you do if the child gets spoiled, then you have to wash it overnight. Hit so badly in the night. In a day if they would have come, might have got smashed completely. Major Kuldip Singh Chandpuri wreaked havoc. Who stood in front of them, Brigadier sir? Brigadier sir started saying brother that it is killing everyone very badly. By then it was morning, and in the morning the Hunter ships did the rest.

The ships that were there at that time were the Hunter ships. This Hunter ship couldn't fly at night but could fly during the day. Throughout the night, Kuldip Singh Chandpuri trashed such to the Pakistanis, gave so much that got bored, so the rest of it was by our Hunter planes. This Hunter plane caused such a terrible panic, Pakistan's tanks totally destroyed in such a terrible war.

Pakistan was blown away so terribly that has no limit. Pakistanis had to flee with their tails tucked in. Brigadier sir ran away and said that run brother run, or these Indian soldiers would take everyone's life. We kept the tank of Pakistan in our museum. Pakistanis ran away leaving their tanks, let's go brother run over from here. It was the fire of 120 Jawans (soldiers).

The situation was like this, the Pakistanis did not come to pick up the dead body of their own fellowmen because of fear, and vultures ate the dead body. We were saying brother, we will not shoot, go away with the corpse. They said you guys turned the desert into a graveyard, we will not come.

So vultures had eaten everything, they did the work of cleaning and all. And Pakistan threatens us; even today they have not improved.

You guys have understood, so now look carefully here. By Pakistan's defeat in Longewala, Pakistan's back was broken in this defeat. And the whole morale of Pakistan was broken. How 120 soldiers washed without soap like this, it was so terrible. They started on the 3rd and we washed them on the 4th.

Now just the Navy got left, the Navy said that brother you gave the Army a chance and gave a chance to the Air Force. The Army washed at night, the Air Force washed in the morning and will we not get a chance to wash? We will wash too. When did the Navy arrive? The Navy reached Karachi on 5 December 1971 and reached Karachi and destroyed Karachi. Such a terrible bombardment was done in Karachi, for some days there was a fire on the Karachi port. The Navy blew up the Karachi port, West Pakistan's back broke.

What condition our Navy did at that time? As much as Pakistan's ship can be found, whose ship is this when it comes to know that brother, this ship belongs to Pakistan, and we demolished it.

Brother is this the way we should do; the child should be beaten like a child. India's Navy has also crossed the limit, is this the way we should?

The entire Karachi port of Pakistan was blown up. It's only been two days since the war started. Hold your heart now; the war is going to be long. They started on December 3rd; we washed the Longewala on December 4th, now Karachi on 5th December.

Now Pakistan thought to destroy India's most dangerous ship which was INS Vikrant. To destroy INS Vikrant, it did send PNS Ghazi. Ghazi was a submarine, he was ordered to kill whom? To Vikrant because if Vikrant's ship had sunk then at that time we would have had a lot of difficulty in winning the war. So how did this Ghazi sink, we killed it with a bad ship.

Now the Indian Army what they did in the East, understand it carefully. This Mukti Bahini who was killing Pakistani soldiers inside Bangladesh, making them ran in the streets because these Pakistani soldiers raped there and murdered innocent people. From the boundaries, our Indian Army was supporting Mukti Bahini and our Air Force from above.

They were devastated and there was no place for them to run away. And out of this, their biggest headache became the Indian Navy. Because when East Pakistan would get the help from West Pakistan, it would be available only through the sea route. And will not go direct from India because on the way the Air Force will kill. West Pakistan was helped from the Navy itself because their soldiers were fighting; supply of food and other things was ruined by INS Vikrant. INS Vikrant was a very big ship of that time of these South East Asia countries. It was such a big ship that aircrafts used to fly over it. That Air Force used to shoot bombs from here, missiles and heavy ships from above. Helicopter was flying so that Mukti Bahini did not face any problem.

Our Vikrant destroyed the Chittagong harbor. Now look at Bangladesh, it was East Pakistan at that time, Chittagong was a big center of the Pakistani Navy at that time. Now Mukti Bahini was not facing any special problem. Now Pakistan said that in any case, destroy this Vikrant.

What was the order given to PNS Ghazi, brother you have to go and drown this Vikrant after going to the Bay of Bengal? Now the people of Pakistan did not have such a good day. The Indian Intelligence Agency came to know that Pakistan's submarine that runs inside the sea is called silent killer. Pakistan's submarine has moved from West Pakistan to the Bay of Bengal. It moved from the Arabian Sea to the Bay of Bengal. Now it was necessary to save Vikrant, so we hid Vikrant, gave some security. PNS means Pakistan Naval Ship, it came to kill whom? Vikrant.

If anyone could have drowned this PNS Ghazi, it was INS Rajput.

At that time there was a problem with INS Rajput. There was some fault in the engine of this Rajput and it got damaged and it was being built at Visakhapatnam, was being repaired, the engine itself got messed up. So here the Indians thought, why don't we call PNS Ghazi, where? At Visakhapatnam. So people said that brother will it come to Visakhapatnam and say kill us, INS Rajput. See how it will come, Indians knew that there would be some spies of Pakistan's in India and they would be giving news from moment to moment to Pakistan. What did the Indians do, all the officers of INS Vikrant were told that you call your home that we are going to Visakhapatnam. We have got a holiday and will stay in Visakhapatnam for ten days; you should prepare food and drink well for us.

Those people had spread the news from the boys that at Visakhapatnam you guys go away, a big ship is coming. Huge ship Vikrant is arriving here, you guys evacuate INS Vikrant is arriving. What was done here? Ordered a lot of fruits, vegetables, eggs, bread, brother this is going for such a big ship that needs 6 months food.

This news spread like fire to Pakistanis and it was reported in Pakistan that brother INS Vikrant is at Visakhapatnam. Yamraj (Death God) was waiting for the death of PNS Ghazi at Visakhapatnam.

PNS Ghazi it turned to where? Visakhapatnam. The ship INS Rajput was waiting quietly at Visakhapatnam, so it came in the water. And INS Rajput saw that it had arrived, before PNS Ghazi could destroy, INS Rajput destroyed

PNS Ghazi. After the sinking of PNS Ghazi, Pakistan suffered a great shock.

Pakistan realized that we could never win, because this PNS Ghazi was a very powerful submarine bought from America which no one could sink and we made it sink from that ship which had been damaged, whose engine was bad. The morale of the Indian Army was on the seventh sky and the Pakistanis were getting shattered day by day.

Now the Pakistanis thought what would they do now? So Pakistanis just called America that brother, you do something. Then the US raised the issue in the (United Nation Security Council) saying in it that East Pakistan is being oppressed. At that time, Russia supported us saying what India is doing, is doing right. We veto against this proposal. There are five veto power countries, if someone vetoes, it's canceled. So one more hope of Pakistan died here. Now Pakistan asked America to save us brother. So America sent its most dangerous ship to attack India on behalf of Pakistan, Seventh Fleet.

The Seventh Fleet was so humongous. It did not walk alone; it walked with the entire Army, with the Navy. Why did it come? To drown Vikrant and its size was double that of Vikrant. Vikrant could not stand before this. Now Indira Gandhi remained in tension. Then at that time Indira Gandhi remembered that brother, we have come to an agreement if America can support Pakistan, then Russia will support India.

So India told Russia that brother America sent such a terrible Seventh Fleet, help us. Russia said that who takes tension. Russia sent a nuclear submarine and Russia sent its 40th Fleet.

Russia's 40th Fleet sailed with a full group of ships. Said that brother let us know who will kill you India. And told America directly that brother, if you attack Vikrant then we will consider this attack as an attack on Russia. Vikrant was standing on the Bay of Bengal and Russia's fortieth fleet stood in support. Russia had also told its Air Force from Yemen that brother, you should take care of India. So for the safety of India, so many people and America was looking here with its Seventh Fleet and Britain also sent its fleet named Eagle. So these people came against us to fight. Now we were thinking about the betterment of Bangladesh. And America's 7th Fleet and Britain's Eagle were against us. And we had our own Vikrant and the Russian Air Force and its fortieth fleet was with us. It was completely made a boundary by the fortieth fleet.

The fortieth fleet said that our ship has an automatic missile. If you come here we will kill you like this only. Russia raised its all submarines over the sea so that it can be seen from satellite and other surveillance and this is what happened. Those people were terrified to see such a group of dangerous ships of Russia, so terrified that Britain said we are too late. Britain's Eagle Fleet Tells America's Seventh Fleet Don't Go There, Too Late. Russia has reached first, now it will kill you, you will be destroyed. So the Seventh Fleet threatened that our ship was carrying nuclear bombs. So the fortieth fleet replied that while coming we too carried atomic bombs and it was so much that we thought, will count later. Come let's see who has how much atomic bomb. Russia had a true friendship with us. And here Sheikh Mujibur Rahman's Mukti Bahini was doing its work.

Now India was in a cross war. Pakistan was losing on every front. Lieutenant General Jagjit Singh Arora made a plan to put psychological pressure on Pakistan by the Indian government. They airdropped the Air Force over Dhaka in East Pakistan.

And in the face of those soldiers there were fewer soldiers in it and only effigies were lowered. It was only the Indian Army knowing that the effigy was coming down. But the media spread this news like fire, and in this we would like to thank BBC News with folded hands. And the BBC gave the cover that the Indian Air Force had done 5000 airdrops of Indian soldiers. Now, they will search in streets and kill Pakistanis, asking why you killed our Bangladeshi brothers. And the Mukti Bahini of Bangladesh was likewise behind them of the Pakistanis. Now the whole morale of Pakistanis is broken. Pakistanis ran in the streets for hiding, think everyone was scared by the effigy. In reality these were not soldiers, the effigy was dropped by airdrop. Now those people ran away out of fear.

Now the Air Force saw that this small psychological pressure had such a dangerous effect that the Air Force said that now let's do one thing. The Air Force attacked the house of the Governor of Bangladesh, now he was not in the house, he survived. After escaping, what is fear; see what is called fear, who was their governor AH Malik resigned. Brother if life remains, will do a lot of jobs, resigned out of fear, Governor of East Pakistan.

According to the constituent, the governor would be the owner of that place resigned, think this fear was inside them. The General was our Manekshaw who was given the responsibility of winning Bangladesh and was entrusted with the responsibility of protecting. He spoke to Lt. Gen Niazi of Pakistan and told him that we give you half an hour's time, and you consider in this half an hour whether you surrender or not. If you surrender, we guarantee you that your soldiers will be kept alive.

And if you don't listen to us, see Governor Sir's house is no good, the same will happen to your house. Because if you don't surrender before us, remember we will make our attacks ten times faster and the defeat is all around you.

India wanted to end this war as soon as possible, because it had become an international matter. Now America had taken it on its nose that brother our ship was shot down, PNS Ghazi was his submarine. It was given to Pakistan, 7th Fleet we did not allow him to enter, and America was getting tarnished. Britain's Eagle was not allowed to enter, it was also getting tarnished.

Now people are saying that India is a poor country, it has just become independent; this was our condition in 1971. And all the people were saying that those who were living in poor society shook America, washed Pakistan everywhere.

What can poor Niazi do now? Niazi was given half an hour's time. Remember December 16, 1971, this is the day that destroyed Pakistan in the 13-day war of our history because on December 3, 1971, Pakistan started the war and on December 16, 1971 we made it to surrender from General Niazi. General Niazi signed the surrender before our Lt. Gen Jagjit Singh Arora. He signed at Dhaka Race Course in Bangladesh.

What is the shame of a general of a country, who got his name recorded in the Guinness Book? How to see the people of Pakistan in Guinness Book Bangladesh is a living example of your bravery, 93,000 army. Imagine 93,000 soldiers all over the world have not surrendered till date, 93,000 people surrendered.

They took off their gun and threw it away, throwing away stars, brother we are surrendering. They took off the belt and let the lamp go where you wanted to take it. This is the same Pakistan remember our 120 soldiers had dusted you in Longewala. Only two soldiers were killed in Longewala and you were completely driven away on 4th December only.

Such a huge defeat has happened anywhere in the world till today 93,000 soldiers have surrendered in front of

India. There is a name in the Guinness Book, what can be a happier thing for Pakistan than this, that brother at least name in the Guinness Book? Later we had left them and after this surrender Bangladesh Mukti Bahini had a smile on its face that now Bangladesh became independent. Indira Gandhi's statement was that Dhaka is the independent capital of the independent Bangladesh; happiness was on the face of Bangladeshi people whose sisters' respect was robbed by the soldiers of the same country.

It was Niazi when he was sent as Lieutenant Governor General to Bangladesh; he did not ask what the situation of Bangladesh was. He asked where are the girls who had been raped, where are they show me, that mean he wants to join, this was the situation. Then Mujibur Rahman was freed from Pakistan. India's promise was that we will free Sheikh Mujibur Rahman and make Bangladesh independent, will get them free and fight for their rights. India fulfilled its promise; today Mujibur Rahman's daughter Sheikh Hasina is taking charge of Bangladesh.

The people of Pakistan who used to call Bangladesh that it is not worth anything, these brothers have overtaken Pakistan. Today their muslin cloth, jute and palm oil are famous all over the world. The people of Bangladesh have also come a long way in repairing ships.

After this war, if India wanted, India would have annexed part of West Pakistan. Because in East Pakistan we defeated them and captured 93,000 soldiers alive and we would tell them to vacate Kashmir from here.

Despite this we had shown humanity to Pakistan, what Pakistan gave us in return for this 26/11 attack, attack on Parliament House, attack in Amritsar, bomb blast in Mumbai all this happened. If we wanted, we could have won that time too. You were alive at the mercy of these Great Indian Soldiers.

We all Indians salute to our country's brave warriors. For our whole nation they are the true real heroes.

A true soldier lives for the battle; warriors pay their dues for their motherland with their life not for money but for their motherland unlike Afghanistan soldiers who surrendered even before putting up a fight. Our Indian warriors don't fight for money but fight for protection of their motherland. For them it's their whole life, its do or die. So in a true sense they are real heroes of our motherland.

No matter how much we thank them in this life; it's never going to be enough. We may not be resourced with great technologies, weapons but our determination is ahead of ages.

Respect and Salute to every Soldier but with a message don't mess with my motherland warriors.

CHAPTER TWO

Sam Manekshaw

The Indian army has surrounded you from all sides. Your Air Force is over, you will not get any help from anyone, Chittagong, Chalna, Mongla all ports are blocked, and no one could reach you even by sea. Your future is locked in our hands at the moment. Mukti Bahini and others are ready to take vengeance from you because you have oppressed them so much. Why waste life, don't you want to go home. Don't waste your time, man is not a coward in front of a soldier, and we'll treat you like a soldier.

Who gave this challenge, which shattered the senses of the enemies? This was the greatest general of India, the first Field Marshal of India, the real leader, the people's man, Sam Manekshaw.

Magnanimous Leader

Sam Manekshaw was in the army and went from bottom to top post. On the one hand they needed to be aggressive, but on the other hand how forgiving can a leader be. When Sam Manekshaw was asked in an interview, what was special about you? What was his answer; I have not punished anyone in my whole life. Army and do not punish, court martial in matter, discipline in matter, rule, law. What did he say whenever someone was court martialed? And if the jury decides he is not guilty, I would have signed without taking a minute. And when someone's court martial turns out to be guilty, I would go home with the file and used to read the file a lot, searched to find out where the problem was. It used to be that this is the third witness, he has lied, check it properly. I used to try how not to punish.

When the surrounding authority told him sir, this will end the discipline, how can we run the army. He used to answer, once see their troubles. How many times do they suffer, if you forgive a little, what difference does it make?

I ask you today, are you forgiving, do you give people the liberty to make mistakes. Because in today's world, if you do not give liberty for half the mistakes, then there will never be innovation, will never grow, somebody thought of doing experiment will never break even its barriers and boundaries.

Reverence

Friends, we keep hearing one thing from the time of the old kings and keep reading when a country is defeated, the army of the victorious country makes a lot of mess, loot, terror but which is the worst is the misbehavior with women. Sam knew this, Sam was a true leader, he had a true man in him, what did he say to his soldiers? Remember when a Begum (Woman) appears, put your hand in your pocket quietly, lower your head and remember Sam. The result of his warning became world famous for the respect of the Indian Army towards women.

A question for every business leader, every corporate, every senior management if there is something wrong with women, it may be with wrong gestures, it may be with wrong words, it may be with messy touch. Whether that mess is in promotion, at any place, do you hide such matters? Do you give your support for the right in such cases, no matter how important the person in front is? But you don't compromise with your principal, if you are like this then you are also a transformation leader like Sam Manekshaw.

Valiant

Friends, who is the real leader? A leader is not someone who is good in good situations. A real leader is one who shows leadership and courage in adverse situations and becomes an example in front of people.

Nine bullets did hit him in the Burma war, not one or two 9, when he reached the doctor. The doctor's condition worsened, the doctor said, I cannot proceed until I understand properly what the matter is, and he asked Sam what happened when Sam regained consciousness. What did he answer; nothing was hit by a donkey. When the leader will show so much courage by taking 9 bullets, when this energy level is seen from within the leader, then imagine what spirit will be transmitted in the army.

You in your society, you in your neighborhood where I am leading in an adverse situation, show such courage that people's batteries get charged from you. Because if the leader becomes de-motivated, the leader loses, then there can never be inspiration among those below.

And when this donkey story spread in the army it kept inspiring people for years, years and years. Know what the great thinker Chanakya said if the defeat is in front, if the roads are all closed, then the leader should show that we will win the battle, that sharpness that should be seen on his face because as long as there is courage in the leader, till the same day there is the spirit of the team.

If your business today, your career is going down for whatever reason, if your company is not surviving because of any reason, give confidence to your people that one day we will definitely be successful. That time of success is about to come, telling the small good news in big and telling the biggest bad news by making it smaller.

Sam Manekshaw is the name of the outspoken, brave, cool personality who made the surrender of more than 90,000 soldiers and civilian personnel. Once the Defense Minister asked his opinion about his superior, he said do not do this from next time because today you are asking me about my senior, tomorrow you will ask my junior about me and this is the easiest way to end the discipline.

A man who fears no one, a man who speaks his mind, a man who thinks for the nation first, and a man who believes in winning. If we learn leadership from this person, then maybe we will not lose someplace in life.

Egalitarian

Long after the 1971 war, once Sam Manekshaw went on a visit to Pakistan, he was well received; he was invited to the governor's house for a meal. What do the people say, sir we know when thousands of our soldiers were arrested, and you gave the Quran (the holy book of Muslims) for everyone to read. Sir had made the best arrangement for our food; maybe we do not have such an arrangement here. And the biggest thing sir, the soldiers here told us that tears fell from our eyes. Your soldiers used to sleep on the ground, but the soldiers who were arrested used to sleep on the bed. Sir no one can be a leader like you.

Friends ask a big question, the way we live, the way we play our career. Normally what we do, we treat the one who treats us better, we respect those who respect us, and we treat those who treat us well. But giving so much respect to the soldiers of the enemy country, giving them a chance to live life in this way, this can be done by a true leader. The leader who has an internal standard, whose internal benchmark is so high that he can say I don't care what the person in front of me is doing, I'll deal with what's my level.

Today I have a question whether it should be family or business, maybe somewhere people have done you wrong, it may be that you have been harmed because of people, you have to look down. Are you carrying the burden, you will keep looking for opportunities to misbehave with

such people or you will ignore them because you have
your own standard.

Self-Confident

Friends, read this story very carefully because all the people who want big success in top or middle management of a company or are you yourself in a big corporate, that's a big question for your leadership. In 1971, the Prime Minister Indira Gandhi called Sam one day and asked Sam in April we want to attack Pakistan are we ready and was very angry. If someone else would have been subordinated they would have been buried. But Sam replied immediately no, if we attack East Pakistan now then our defeat is certain. On hearing this Indira Gandhi got angry before she said anything further, what was Sam's answer, mam tell me how to send my resignation on the health ground, mental ground or on physical ground.

And Indira Gandhi understood this and controlled her anger and asked when will you be ready? Tell me when you're ready; Sam finished the fight in just 13 days. Are you a yes man, is something wrong going on in your company then you say yes to your boss or do you dare to tell the truth to your boss.

Do you give each other support by making the company a success, does your personal interest become a hurdle in the company's interest and docs your personal interest come above the interest of the society? A true leader is the one who puts his/her interest behind, puts the team's interest in front of him/her, then the interest of the company, then the interest of the society, and above all the interest of the country. That is why we salute a leader like Ratan Tata.

Sam Manekshaw's Leadership as a leader raises the big question, he could have been scared at that time that I may lose my position, and I may lose my seniority. But regardless of his position, he answered what was right for the country. The day when you think for the country, for the society, and for the company's bigger goal, you will start thinking for the team first, that day you will be called a true leader.

Enigmatic

Another interesting anecdote that caused hyper energy communication in the army for a long time. A soldier was injured, his motivation was very low and he was depressed as three bullets hit him. Sam Manekshaw came to him, put a hand on his shoulder said soldier I got 9 bullets and I became the Commander-in-Chief of this country, he stated hey you have got just three bullets get ready soon, many more fights have to be fought and a fire broke out inside the soldier and when this incident spread, there was a fire all around. Friends, when the leader is so inspiring, when the leader is not ready to give up, when the leader is not ready to bow down, when leaders aim to blow big problems like this then the leader who generates the energy, the inspiration, the motivation then there is no match for him/her.

Unprejudiced

What is the greatest quality of a leader? Global Research says appreciation and encouragement to see the good in its people. Well answer one more question, which is India's most fearless defense squad? Who doesn't know Gorkha's squad, Gorkha regiment is the bravest regiment.

But let's go back to history; this regiment has been doing service since the time of the British, earlier it was headed by British officers. When all the British officers were gone, Sam Manekshaw became its chief. Sam Manekshaw was so appreciative for this regiment and so mastered in his appreciation that he said the line which became the quote which was different. What did he say? He said that if someone says that he is not afraid of dying, either he is lying or he is a Gorkha. He loved so much true appreciation, so much frank appreciation for two Gurkha regiments. If he could not choose between the two, he used to wear both badges. Can you be impartial as a leader, can you as a leader what is my religion, what is my caste, what is my province, what is my language, instead of being biased towards those people, you can praise those who are right.

If you can do that you will be remembered for years as a true leader and if you give priority to people who are buttering you and speak sweetly in front of you, you will be forgotten very quickly as a leader.

Associate

Many leaders want to tie crown their heads with success and always want to uncrown their heads in defeat. And when it came to having respect there, Indira Gandhi told Sam to go and get the respect. You know what Sam replied, Sam said the leader of Eastern Commander is Arora. And if he goes to get this stuff then it will be right, such a big war is one of the biggest wars in the history of India. Surrender of 93,000 soldiers but did not tie crown to his heads, recommended to the entitled person who was leading that region.

As a leader we have a big question do we give credit to our team, do we give credit to the people who help us win. In the family too, have we made our parents, our siblings, and others do we give them credit?

Who is the real leader? The real leader is the one who when he wins says because of others and when he/she lose, say it was my fault.

CHAPTER THREE

APJ Abdul Kalam

"Dreams are not those that come in sleep
Dreams are those that do not let you sleep"

The son of the boatman of Rameshwaram, whose verses of the Gita resonated in one ear and Darwin's principles in the other ear.

His father's boat used to take the pilgrims to the temple of Rameshwaram and when the pilgrims used to circumambulate Rameshwaram. During that time, he used to study the principles of physics.

Not only me or you, the people who are spread will also talk about Dr. APJ Abdul Kalam, the favorite of the whole country.

Avul-Great grandfather name

Pakir-Grandfather name

Jainulabdeen-Father name

Abdul Kalam his own name

11th President 2002 to 2007, People's President.

An Englishman asked in the conference about Abdul Kalam, tell me in one sentence. There a child replied, simple Indian inexplicable, his specialty cannot be defined.

Once a child asked him what the mantra to be successful is, he said four things have to be done. Four things to be successful make a strong aim, for that aim keep acquiring all the knowledge, keep acquiring the knowledge you need for that. Third, hard work and fourth persevere do not give up.

Live life like this
Even after the end of life
People remember you for life

He was born on 15 October 1931, in Rameshwaram (Tamil Nadu). He was born in a Muslim family. His father was a boatman by profession and his father was not very educated, so he has suffered a lot from the beginning.

Family was very big, there were 10 siblings and there was a shortage of money. So to meet his expenses, he started selling newspapers at a young age, he knew that he would get money but while selling it all along the way he used to go through all the newspapers.

When he was eight years old, he was very young, some kilometers away from his village; a sir used to teach very good mathematics and said that at four in the morning, one hour class was free. I will teach the child who will take a bath at four o'clock in the morning and come.

He would be ready at three o'clock in the morning to take a bath with cold water whether it was winter, rain or storm; he used to reach at four o'clock.

When Kalam went to study, he had a lantern on his support; he had only two hours of oil that was ignited with kerosene oil. But when father and mother saw he was interested in studying, they kept their darkness for themselves and did it till 11 o'clock.

Never be afraid of hard work, never shy away from honesty. Setting a small goal is a sin, that's why, always dream of a great goal. When he was in class V, his teacher Mr. Subhas Subramaniam was teaching children how birds fly, kids didn't understand, so he took them from there to the seaside and showed the bird flying there and there he showed the live example of the bird flying. The detail was understood of the wings, so his profession was shaped from there in his mind. His house was close to the sea and desires were ahead of the sky, from where he developed interest in aeronautics.

He completed high school at Schwartz Higher Secondary School in Ramanathapuram. And one day once in school, he got into the wrong class and the teacher scolded him. As long as you do not understand this which is your class, you have reached the wrong class in mathematics class so what will you study and what will you go on and at the same time, he studied so much in mathematics that he got 100 marks out of 100, teacher was surprised.

**"If you wanna shine like the sun
So first burn like the sun"**

Wanted to fly in the sky since childhood, that's why he joined the highest college in Madras, the best college in the country MIT (Madras Institute of Technology). There he took an entry in aeronautical engineering. Now there was aeronautics in the college, so the project was to design the aircraft. Now he started making the design of the aircraft and the design which was made was shown to the teacher. The teacher didn't like it and the teacher said if you can't make a good design Abdul Kalam then your scholarship will be taken back, his mind was blown. Hearing this from the teacher, the ground slipped under his feet.

He told the teacher to give me a month's time; I will give a very nice design. The teacher said that there is no one month, just three days. His mind was shaken at that time. He was scared that the scholarship should not be snatched away.

He told the teacher to give me a month's time; I will give a very nice design. The teacher said that there is no one month, just three days. His mind was shaken at that time. He was scared that the scholarship should not be snatched away.

"The one who wins over sleep and slander
No one can stop them from moving forward"

After this, he passed the exam with a good number. Now his studies are done. What is the next learning from life, failure should not be allowed in the heart and success should not enter the head, control heart and mind.

After this, he passed the exam with a good number. Now his studies are done. What is the next learning from life, failure should not be allowed in the heart and success should not enter the head, control heart and mind.

Those who had to be selected in the Air Force there, now out of 25 seats, 8 were vacant and his rank came 9, fell behind by a number, eight people got selected. When he got down from Dehradun, he visited to Rishikesh, he went to Rishikesh. There he met Swami Sivananda, Swami Sivananda was very popular. So when he went to Sivananda and told his problem, then Swami Sivananda told him to read the Gita and told him that if the desire comes out of your heart is pure and if you have faith in it then there is a strange power in it, that's why what you have thought will happen, you believe. This is the learning of Gita. Where you have remembrance and feeling you will become ripe like this. After that when he returned to Delhi after meeting his guru and then the job of the Ministry of Defense was left, DRDO. Who knew the same DRDO would be most effective in taking the country forward? He was promoted and he came in the team of Dr. Vikram Sarabhai.

Dr. APJ Abdul Kalam was patriotic, not opportunistic. Abdul Kalam was a special person. In 1963, he was selected from the team of Vikram Sarabhai to send him to NASA, for training. He went to NASA for 6 months of training, America's largest organization in which he wanted to move forward.

NASA was shocked to see, said man this boy is very tremendous and you are very champion. Brother, listen to me we will give you American citizenship, salary five times more than India, get married to white girl and live a comfortable life. In his autobiography, he said that once in his mind he thought whether I should stay here or not. Lot of choices whether to move towards ideals or embrace the opportunity of garland. He thought that he would not go abroad for money and love, and would not miss this opportunity of the country, so he came back to the country.

Difficulty will always come in the way of your success. The next story came with a lot of difficulties when he joined Scientist Team ISRO from the very beginning, what he said was real problems are different and inconvenience is different. Problems and inconvenience are different, different things.

He did not pay attention to the inconvenience in his life, paid attention to the real problems. The inconvenience came a lot, because he had joined ISRO in the initial days. The bigger the difficulties in life and if you overcome them, the bigger your name will be.

When he joined in the initial days, nothing was given and there was no investment there. St. Mary's Church became his office. There all the scientists, engineers who had come from NASA after training were sitting in the church office. They built rocket launch pad by the seaside and in the cowshed laboratory was built there.

On a cycle and on a bullock cart, slowly, slowly, or on a bicycle, the rocket's tiny, tiny parts and satellites were carried.

They launched the first sounding rocket in 1963 in the midst of all difficulties. At that time he was 32 years old, his engagement had been fixed, he kept working, and he was dreaming about the country's first rocket and forgot to go to his engagement. Abdul Kalam was engaged in making rockets for the country. Don't think that while going through a phase in life, this life will always be difficult; this trouble has come and will also go away. He had caught the Gita in the hand, which was given to him by his guru.

In 1969 when he was given the command of the director of ISRO, he thought about SLV-3 (satellite launch vehicle) and which goes to its orbit and sets. When they did not have money, what did he say there, will work for SLV-3 and we will work for PSLV too. For which he asked for funds from the government.

In publically Indira Gandhi said that the fund is not there, but privately gave him a little fund. And after getting a little funding, he got busy with his project. Now Abdul Kalam used to work for 18 hours a day, 365 days a year and 366 days in leap years. From 1969 to 1979, he put his heart and soul for 10 years; he only took two leaves once at the death of his father and once at the death of his mother, no rest days, no Saturday or Sunday, August 15th, nor January 26th. His SLV-3 launch failed in 1979, despite 10 years of hard work.

And when it failed, he got very nervous because at that time the whole country was watching it. The media of the whole world was watching them. He had become frustrated and in the situation his professor Satish Dhawan, who was the chairman at that time he called Abdul Kalam and said media, is waiting go there and talk.

Kalam was nervous. Now every blame will be on him because he was this Mission Director and was the Project Director, as a Mission Director Project Director because of his failure now the whole world was watching his failure and when Satish Dhawan called him, got more nervous.

Now what will I answer to the media, the media said that you have ruined the country by wasting crores of rupees, what right did you have? And there Professor Satish Dhawan took the mic and what did he say, this team is very tremendous. It failed for the first time, within a year the same team will launch this SLV-3 again and he doubled the energy inside the team. Abdul Kalam was surprised to see that he took his failures on himself. Worked hard again for a year, intelligence was perfect and this time when SLV-3 became successful. After that, Professor Satish Dhawan gave the mic this time in Kalam's hand, said now you have been successful now you will answer, Abdul Kalam was surprised and said this is called leadership.

When I succeed, I will give credit to the team and when I fail I will take all the failures. Impressed by this, Indira Gandhi saw that both of them did tremendous work. She told Professor Dhawan she wanted to meet Abdul Kalam. He told Abdul Kalam, Indira Gandhi wants to meet brother, Abdul Kalam said brother I do not have suits, I am roaming in torn flip-flops. How can I come and meet in front of her? So he said that brother, you are already wearing a suit of success, don't want a suit of clothes.

He was very impressed when he went there and met Indira Gandhi. She said that now you will have to do more work in defense, in this situation China and Pakistan today everyone is preparing for missiles. You make missiles for our country and at the same time Atal Bihari Vajpayee had his first meeting. When he proceeded to meet Atalji, Atalji did not shake hands with him, Atalji hugged him. Indira Gandhi smiled and said, pay attention Atalji he is a Muslim. Atalji said that he is Muslim later, first he is a citizen of our country and he is a great scientist of our country, Abdul Kalam smiled at him.

Success was being achieved, for that he was getting reward too in 1981, he was awarded Padma Bhushan. He was made director of DRDO in 1982.

He had reached his main post but he was not happy from his heart. He knew that China and Pakistan were making missiles on missiles and they were seeing the security of the country in danger. Abdul Kalam was inspired by the story of Barbarik in the Mahabharata. The story of Barbarik was different, Barbarik would say that he has three arrows, and what he will do with three arrows, will protect everyone in the first arrow, whom to attack in the second and the game over in the third arrow.

From there he developed the Integrated Guided Missile Program. Why don't we make such a missile that if a man runs to the left, the missile goes to the left, if a man runs to the right, the missile goes to the right and if the tank that you want to blow up if the tank goes ahead, then the missile will go ahead? How to make Guided Missiles was imaginative from this episode of Barbarik.

He said in an interview that Lord Krishna got the blessings of Sudarshan Chakra. Lord's Sudarshan Chakra is very remote controlled. Brother when Krishna leaves the Sudarshan Chakra it will go and stop first, for as long as he has to talk is wandering around. And when you finished saying it, then struck and came back, then he said this is a big system. There was a lot of advanced technology, so from there they started this model of Integrated Guided Missile and after that they planted missiles one after the other.

He used to give lectures in every college about imagination. In 1985, he launched a missile named Trishul. Then he launched the Prithvi missile in 1989, now he was behind Agni. He made Akash, Nag. To make the Agni missile he was facing problems, the fire was spreading again and again. The Agni missile was a big important project but now across the country people had different meaning of it according to their own, and they were very serious because of people's questions again and again. Before the end of the same 89, he succeeded Agni.

"The biggest success is not to lose enthusiasm when you fail again and again."

They were watching all the other powerful countries, they were launching missiles, and how could they attack on other continents? Release missiles from India to reach Europe, reach America, and reach other continents. Everyone made great preparations, when they launched Agni in 89; India was the 6th country after Russia, USA, China, France, UK and who made so many powerful missiles.

Understand my point; it was Abdul Kalam who made India stand on the 6th rank putting other countries behind. They used to say that they do not have to use missiles, but they have to show their great form or not. After the 10th chapter when Lord Krishna saw Arjun yawning. If Arjun is not taking it seriously, then I should show vast form and Krishna showed vast form, Krishna did not kill. Arjun came on track seeing vast form. That's why sometimes when Pakistan and China show us eyes, just show the vast form. We will not leave the missile, just show the vast form it will automatically come on the line, this thing is understood.

So Abdul Kalamji made it strong, his hard work paid off in 1993 when he also succeeded PSLV. Today it is the gift of Kalam that PSLV completed the journey till Mars even at a low cost in 2014. We have traveled to Mars in less than what it costs for a Hollywood movie. In 2017, it was Abdul Kalam, due to which 104 satellites were launched with one rocket, the cheapest affordable program in the world. This is the gift of Abdul Kalam.

It was the same Kalam in 1979, it was the same India, and no country was helping. And today in 2017 it is Kalam's gift when countries from all over the world came to India, asking to send our satellite in your rocket; we helped Netherland, Switzerland, Israel, Kazakhstan. We had sent 104 satellites; it was Abdul Kalam's gift.

The conversation of nuclear power all over the world was happening; they saw that brother America was also giving threats. Now the thing is that it is inauspicious to be afraid of threats and the one who has done anything for the country is a true Hindustani (Indian).

Sir Kalam was a true Hindustani (Indian). He adopted three tricks, first scientists were put in army uniform, so that satellites do not recognize and consider them as normal army who are roaming around. Whenever they will do any work, they will do it in the middle of the time when one satellite will go and the second one is about to come. He used to prepare at that time and after the work was over, they used to make the ground very clear. When the satellite would come back, it would not know that something has happened here, the army men are roaming freely.

America did not come to know from 1992 to 1997, they did a lot of work continuously. Nearby villages and other people also did not know what happened here and this effort brought their color. In 1998, India did a nuclear test in the name of Operation Shakti, today due to these efforts India has become nuclear rich. There were 5 countries at that time: America, the UK, France, Russia, and China, these were 5 countries. We were not bothered by anyone; we had problems with China because China was quietly giving nuclear power to Pakistan at that time. Here India has completed its efforts, due to his constant efforts; he was given Bharat Ratna Award in 1997. He served India for 41 years. He retired in 1999, in those days Atalji was going in action here, he called Abdul Kalam. We want to give the ministry to you, come here you are a wise man. Abdul said I will tell after a day. A day later Kalam called and said I want to refuse and he went to meet and said that I should prepare a new generation which will make India a world guru.

To prepare a new generation I want to teach in colleges, back to Annamalai University Tamil Nadu for my teaching profession. The next time when the time came to become the President of India somewhere in 2002, the name of the people came, many things happened back and forth. So again Atalji called, Kalamji picked up the call, then Atalji said, look this is a request now don't tell like last time, then Kalamji said what is the request, Atalji said, we have your name recommendation to become the President of the country. We want to give, just say yes, Kalamji smiled and said, give me one hour's time. He went back after an hour and he called again and accepted okay I am ready for this.

Now the coronation of Kalamji was to be done like the coronation of Lord Ram. After 14 years of exile when Lord Rama came back and at the time of his consecration, his brother asked whom you want to call. Lord Ram said that I was not here in 14 years; I do not have friends here and those who are our friends, you all know and that you must have invited them all and then Lord Ram said yes, but during this exile, I made a friend, the one in those days a boatman who helped us cross the river, that boatman has helped us a lot, he is our friend call that boatman and bring him in the coronation, (boatman) was called in the coronation of Lord Rama. In the same way when Abdul Kalamji was asked that now yours too coronation is going to happen, you are going to be the President of India and Kalamji said that everyone who had to be called, I am sure has been called I have only two friends, when I used to live in the South, at that time a cobbler who used to repair my torn shoes, he has helped me a lot and my another friend call him, dhaba man who fed him food, sometimes even two extra rotis, said that both of them must be called.

If someone becomes President, then he/she goes to Rashtrapati Bhavan with a truck and goes out with multiple extra trucks. But Abdul Kalamji was the only President who had gone to the building with two suitcases and while leaving came back from the building with only two suitcases. What was in his net worth was nothing, a paternal house in Rameshwaram that his father had built, 2500 books, a veena which he used to play with great pleasure, wrist watch, and a CD player in which he used to recite hymns. There was a laptop, 6 shirts of which three were given by DRDO and 3 of his own, 4 pants two of which were given by DRDO and two of his own. There were 3 suits and a pair of shoes, yes but what was special about them 40 doctorates, never studied PhD himself, and did not study any medical PhD.

But the university he went to, people used to give him doctorates, law, engineering, science, so many types of doctorates, Padma Bhushan, Padma Vibhushan, Bharat Ratna, Veer Savarkar Award, and Ramanujan Award.

I would like to tell one particular thing about him, although he was a Muslim but he was a vegetarian. His great love was for animals. He used to say animals are angels with fur; they are a symbol of the environment. If they are in trouble then understand that our bad days are not far away.

Once upon a time what used to be their boundary? Somebody told them to put glass pieces for security, and then he said absolutely not, it can be very harmful for the birds, he refused. And at the time when he became the President while walking in the Rashtrapati Bhavan Mughal Garden, he saw a peacock that was neither able to open its mouth nor close it, he called the veterinary doctor and saw that there is a tumor in the peacock's neck, they treated him. A leader's kindness is revealed by the fact that he is helping those who can't give him anything in return. When a leader helps people who can't give anything in return, that's the sign of a great leader.

Abdul Kalamji has touched many hearts; he used to believe in nationalism. He is a man of principle and therefore he is always respected everywhere. Kalam once invited the whole family because he did not have any family, he used to live alone in Rashtrapati Bhavan and once when the whole family was called in Rashtrapati Bhavan.

So those people stayed for 8 days and the whole family had 10 siblings, a total of 52 people and Kalamji saw a lot of expenses. So he started keeping the account even for the cup of tea, all the people were sent to Ajmer Sharif by private bus and he kept the account of it too. He made all the calculations with his accountant and said how much it was made, then he said 3, 52,000 Rs, he deducted from his salary and he said that the responsibility of Rashtrapati Bhavan is only of the President and not of the entire family.

Abdul Kalamji was such a humble person. Humility is a royal pride without a crown. The kindness of a great person is his humility. Kalam was once invited as the chief guest at IIT BHU, there were 7 chairs, and the middle chair was high? The middle chair was high because he was the president and he had to sit. He said move the chair and put the equal chair. They said no sir; this is a special chair for our chief guest. So he understood who the chief guest was, brother who is a great teacher in education. So he told the Vice Chancellor to sit on the big chair, the Vice Chancellor got nervous and said but you are President and this is for you. They removed the big chair and placed the same sized chair, Kalam was like this.

It is said that no paternal property given by mother and father can make you as rich as honesty. The richest person is the one who is honest; the whole world is standing with you.

Kalamji at the age of 70, he got the Youth Icon of the Year Award. He did not retire at the age of 83, he re-tried. He was not tired, he was inspired. He was not tired up, he was fired up. His eyesight was decreasing but they were engaged in illuminating the lives of the youth. The speed of the steps of his body had decreased, but he was engaged in increasing the speed of the country's prosperity.

An extraordinary, unique and supernatural person has left us forever in 2015 while delivering the last lecture inside Shillong of the same IIM, as a warrior attains martyrdom on his battlefield similarly, immediately after giving lectures inside IIM Shillong, while giving lectures there. What was yesterday is not today, what is today will not be tomorrow, in the same way there will be no other Kalam in this universe. Countries like Switzerland celebrate his birthday 15th October as World's Science Day. It becomes the definition of goods of India, when it comes to Mr. A.P.J. Abdul Kalam.

CHAPTER FOUR

Veer Maratha Chhatrapati Shivaji

Chhatrapati Shivaji was born on 19 February 1630. Father Shahaji Raje Bhosale and mother Jijabai Shahaji.

Father Shahaji Bhosale at that period was serving Mughal's, so he was not available most. So Shivaji's mother Jijabai was the one who spent most time with Chhatrapati Shivaji. Shivaji in his early childhood was taught about Mahabharata, Ramayana, and Bhagavad Gita by his mother Jijabai, which influenced Chhatrapati Shivaji from his early childhood that he developed natural leadership in him.

Though he was small, there was a Maval named place which was located near Pune. The people of Maval were very brave; there Shivaji lived for 3 years with people and wandered in the jungle. There he saw that these people have a lot of strengths but these are unguided missiles. One day he gathered his friends and villagers and he said Marathas are known as Mughals slave and this slavery is mindset and nothing. It is a state of mind. Marathas have to break this slavery from Mughals.

From Nizam Shah and Adil Shah, Marathas ought to be freed from their capture, he prepared the villagers. There he took out his knife and from his blood, he put tilak on

Shivling. And there he stated that I will do Swaraj Yatra.

Slavery is state of mind. To free Marathas from slavery mindset, he had small team, not much manpower, not much resource, not much funds, there was not much support from backend, no alliance too.

So he started very intelligently, I believe our country should know that Chhatrapati Shivaji was a combination of great warrior and intelligent as Chanakya. Chhatrapati Shivaji was good in Guerilla Warfare, which is called Ganimi Kava. In such a small age such intelligent, Ganimi (Enemy) Kava (Tactics) which means to fool your enemy with tactics. Chhatrapati Shivaji used to fight with such tactics which enabled to spread his empire from south to Gujarat and further far states.

Mughals King, Adil Shah captured the father of Chhatrapati Shivaji and jailed. Chhatrapati Shivaji for many days was thinking what to do, at that time **only** Shahjahan was also in Delhi where Chhatrapati Shivaji influenced and convinced Shahjahan to help in releasing his father. Chhatrapati Shivaji was master of alliance.

Maharaj Chhatrapati Shivaji has won many battles without even fighting. For him winning was more important than fighting. This is called making surrender beforc the sword comes out. His intelligence was such that he made alliances with enemies.

From Konkan Coastline, which was from Gujarat, Maharashtra, Goa, Karnataka where he build the Navy Force. Chhatrapati Shivaji is also known as father of the Indian Navy.

Chhatrapati Shivaji won Pratapgarh. Within 18 days Fort of Panhal was also captured.

Mirza Raja Jai Singh defeated Shivaji and signed the treaty of Purandhar, losing 23 forts in the treaty. Within a few years won 360 forts. His fight was not against any religion; his fight was for protection of Marathas. His fight was not against Muslim; his fight was against Mughals who came as invaders.

In Chhatrapati Shivaji's period, many Muslims were army generals, even many of his friends were also Muslims. Even his team's wazir-e-azam was also Muslim, his many gurus were also Muslims but he was against Mughals, who mistreated Marathas and made their servants.

The Veer Maratha Chhatrapati Shivaji always showed respect to women. His leadership wisdom came from Mahabharata, Bhagavad Gita, and Ramayan which he also spread in his soldiers. Whereas Mughals used to pick women kidnap, raped, and broke temples. Whereas Chhatrapati Shivaji never disrespected others religion, nor harmed any women, even if my soldier is caught doing wrong I will finish. He was praised for this quality that people were ready to give their life for Chhatrapati Shivaji.

We should not forget our country's great history.

Conclusion

Thank you for reading this Book.